My Santa

A gift from My Santa on Christmas 2008,

Written by **Brandi McDonald Sikes**
Illustrations **by Julia Embrey Mann**

AuthorHouse™
1663 Liberty Drive
Bloomington, IN 47403
www.authorhouse.com
Phone: 833-262-8899

New International Version (NIV)

ISBN: 978-1-4969-1558-0 (sc)
ISBN: 978-1-4969-1557-3 (e)

Library of Congress Control Number: 2014909686

Illustrations copyright © 2014 by Julia Mann
Book Cover design copyright © 2014 by Julia Mann

Print information available on the last page.

Published by AuthorHouse 12/06/2024

author**HOUSE**®

My Santa

Jesus said, "Let the little children come to me, and do not hinder
them, for the kingdom of heaven belongs to such as these."

—Matthew 19:14

Endorsements

"Brandi McDonald Sikes transforms the reader's excitement for Christmas and the love of Santa to the permanent, sustaining love Christ offers all of us. Her book is a wonderful gift for all who want to share this amazing love with their children."

Diane Paddison
Author, "Work, Love, Pray"
Founder, www.4wordwomen.org
Former member of the Global Executive Teams of two
Fortune 500 and one Fortune 1000 companies

"I love how the author has taken the character of Santa to redirect a child's attention to Jesus, the real reason for Christmas. I also loved the bible study and questions included in the book to inspire the adult reader and generate further conversation with the family."

Anita Carman
Author, "Transforming for a Purpose"
Founder, www.inspirewomen.org
Bible Teacher

My Santa

I met Santa at the mall today.
There were bazillions of kids in line!
They all told him what
they wanted for Christmas.
How would he ever
remember mine?

My favorite thing about Santa is
He never leaves anyone out.
But they say he's always watching
When I'm good and when I pout.

As I waited along the
candy cane path,
I counted the kids
and worked on the math.

How can he
put all
those gifts
into flight?

How does he deliver
them all in one night?

I climbed up onto Santa's lap.
He hugged me just the same.
He did not remind me of when I was bad,
And he called me by my name!

I told him about all that I wanted.
He gently listened to me.
All the worries of the world seemed to fade
As I sat upon his knee.

I left excited about my toys
He would soon load up in his sack.
I really enjoyed my time with him.
I wish I could go back.

Santa surprised us at school today.
I recognized his beard.
But something was different about his eyes.
Something was really weird.

As I waited along the candy cane path,
I counted the kids and worked on the math.
How can he put all those gifts into flight?
How does he deliver them all in one night?

At home I questioned on Daddy's lap,
"Santa wasn't quite the same.
Why was his beard all crooked,
And he couldn't remember my name?"

He said, "I understand why you are sad,
But I have good news for you.
Jesus always knows your name
And loves you through and through."[1]

That night, I told Jesus about my troubles.
He gently listened to me.[2]
Worries of this world faded away
As I prayed upon my knees.[3]

The church is glowing with twinkle lights.
Hurray, it's Christmas Eve!
Santa is finally on his way.
It's hard to believe.

I must be in bed, fast asleep.
That's Santa's one condition.
But Mommy always says to me,
"Christmas is more than just tradition."[4]

It's the story of Jesus
We must come to hear.
As I light my own candle,[5]

It all becomes clear.

I love the story of Jesus
Born in a manger,[6]
God's gift to the world.[7]
To me, He's no stranger.

The three kings with gifts
Is my favorite part.
They followed the star
And believed with their hearts.[8]

"May we worship the king?"
They gently asked. "Please."
Can you imagine Mary's response
As they fell to their knees?

They brought gifts like Santa
But in many ways better.[9]
They weren't just responding
To my selfish letter.

As I gaze at the beautiful lights on the tree,
I am reminded my Jesus died there for me.[10]
God's gift to the world is mine to receive.
I now have decided in what I believe.[11]

I still love Santa
Because he reminds me of Jesus.
He's always there with open arms,
Waiting to receive us.[12]

He is a miracle worker.[13]
He never sleeps.[14]
That twinkle in his eye
Is for all of His sheep.[15]

His red suit—
The blood that was shed for me.[16]
Its white trim—
The purity, setting me free.[17]

His gifts—
Like the grace Jesus gives to me.[18]
His mercy—
When I'm not as good as I should be.[19]

His laugh—
Like the joy that springs from my heart
And remains throughout the day.
Jesus never departs.[20]

Long Santa lines are like our prayers;
He makes time for each one.
This is yet another way Santa
Reminds me of God's Son.

Through the hustle and bustle,
One thing is clear.
I traded my Santa for Jesus this year.

I told Jesus these thoughts.
He said, "You finally see.
I'm already waiting,
When you come looking for Me.[21]

"I watch over you always.[22]
Your prayers, I hear.
I shower you with My 'presence'
More than once a year.

"Now that you know Me,
Building your faith is a must.[23]
Enjoy tradition,
But give Me your trust.[24]

"My plan for your life
Is bigger than your dreams.[25]
I will give you My joy,
The tougher life seems.[26]

"I love the way My birthday
Is celebrated on earth.
But I'm sad My death is not valued
As much as My birth.[27]

"Through the hustle and bustle
That comes again next year,
I need you to invite
More children to hear.[28]

"The truth about Santa
Will cause them to see.
Every Christmas party
Is really about Me.[29]

"I will give you My strength[30]
To show them the way
To have Christmas morning
Each and every day."

Bible Study

1. Read Hebrews chapter 11, verse 6.

> And without faith it is impossible to please God, because anyone who comes to
> him must believe that he exists and that he rewards those who earnestly seek him.
> —Hebrews 11:6

    a. The wise men traveled for many days to see the baby Jesus. Do you think they believed Jesus was real?

    b. What would you travel a long way to see?

    c. How far would you go to see what you want to see?

    d. How do think the wise men felt when they finally saw Jesus?

    e. Do you believe that God exists?

    f. What does the Bible say God will do for those who believe He exists (Hebrews 11:6)?

    g. What is the greatest reward you have ever received?

    h. Who gave the reward to you and why?

    i. Because God is greater than anyone on earth who can give you a reward, how big can His rewards be?

2. Read John chapter 20, verse 29.

> Then Jesus told him, "Because you have seen me, you have believed;
> blessed are those who have not seen and yet have believed."
> —John 20:29

a. Could the wise men see Jesus when they were on their journey?

b. What could the wise men see (Matthew 2:1)?

c. Can you see God?

d. What can you see at Christmastime that reminds you of Jesus?

(Endnotes)

1   Isaiah 43:1: "But now, this is what the LORD says—he who created you, O Jacob, he who formed you, O Israel: 'Fear not, for I have redeemed you; I have summoned you by name; you are mine.'"

2   Matthew 7:7–8: "Ask and it will be given to you; seek and you will find; knock and the door will be opened to you. For everyone who asks receives; he who seeks finds; and to him who knocks, the door will be opened."

3   1 John 4:4: "You, dear children, are from God and have overcome them, because the one who is in you is greater than the one who is in the world." 1 John 5:5: "Who is it that overcomes the world? Only he who believes that Jesus is the Son of God."

4   Colossians 2:8: **"See to it that no one takes you captive through hollow and deceptive philosophy, which depends on human tradition and the basic principles of this world rather than on Christ."**

5   John 8:12: "When Jesus spoke again to the people, he said, 'I am the light of the world. Whoever follows me will never walk in darkness, but will have the light of life.'"

6   Luke 2:7: "And [Mary] gave birth to her firstborn, a son. She wrapped him in cloths and placed him in a manger, because there was no room for them in the inn."

7   John 3:16: **"For God so loved the world that he gave his one and only Son,** that whoever believes in him shall not perish but have eternal life."

8   Matthew 2:1–2: "After Jesus was born in Bethlehem in Judea, during the time of King Herod, Magi from the east came to Jerusalem and asked, 'Where is the one who has been born king of the Jews? We saw his star in the east and have come to worship him.'"

9   Matthew 2:11: "On coming to the house, they saw the child with his mother Mary, and they bowed down and worshiped him. Then they opened their treasures and presented him with gifts of gold and of incense and of myrrh."

10   John 19:17–18: "Carrying his own cross, he went out to the place of the Skull (which in Aramaic is called Golgotha). Here they crucified him, and with him two others—one on each side and Jesus in the middle."

11   John 5:24: "I tell you the truth, whoever hears my word and believes him who sent me has eternal life and will not be condemned; he has crossed over from death to life."

12   Luke 15:20: "So he got up and went to his father. But while he was still a long way off, his father saw him and was filled with compassion for him; he ran to his son, threw his arms around him and kissed him."

13   John 20:30–31: "Jesus did many other miraculous signs in the presence of his disciples, which are not recorded in this book. But these are written that you may believe that Jesus is the Christ, the Son of God, and that by believing you may have life in his name."

14   John 5:17: "Jesus said to them, 'My Father is always at his work to this very day, and I, too, am working.'"

15   Psalm 95:7: "For he is our God and we are the people of his pasture, the flock under his care."

16   Colossians 1:19–21: "For God was pleased to have all his fullness dwell in him, and through him to reconcile to himself all things, whether things on earth or things in heaven, by making peace through his blood, shed on the cross."

17   Hebrews 9:13–14: "The blood of goats and bulls and the ashes of a heifer sprinkled on those who are ceremonially unclean sanctify them so that they are outwardly clean. How much more, then, will

the blood of Christ, who through the eternal Spirit offered himself unblemished to God, cleanse our consciences from acts that lead to death, so that we may serve the living God!"

18   Matthew 7:11: "If you, then, though you are evil, know how to give good gifts to your children, how much more will your Father in heaven give good gifts to those who ask him!"

19   Titus 3:4–6: "But when the kindness and love of God our Savior appeared, he saved us, not because of righteous things we had done, but because of his mercy. He saved us through the washing of rebirth and renewal by the Holy Spirit, whom he poured out on us generously through Jesus Christ our Savior …"

20   Deuteronomy 31:6: "Be strong and courageous. Do not be afraid or terrified because of them, for the Lord your God goes with you; he will never leave you nor forsake you."

21   Jeremiah 29:14a: ""I will be found by you," declares the LORD,…"

22   Psalm 32:8: "I will instruct you and teach you in the way you should go; I will counsel you and watch over you."

23   Luke 8:25: "He got up and rebuked the wind and the raging waters; the storm subsided, and all was calm. 'Where is your faith?' he asked his disciples. In fear and amazement they asked one another, 'Who is this? He commands even the winds and the water, and they obey him.'"

24   Proverbs 3:5: "Trust in the LORD with all your heart and lean not on your own understanding; in all your ways acknowledge him, and he will make your paths straight."

25   1 Corinthians 2:9: "However, as it is written: 'No eye has seen, no ear has heard, no mind has conceived what God has prepared for those who love him.'"

26   Psalm 94:18–19: "When I said, 'My foot is slipping,' your love, O LORD, supported me. When anxiety was great within me, your consolation brought joy to my soul."

27   Luke 16:15: "He said to them, 'You are the ones who justify yourselves in the eyes of men, but God knows your hearts. What is highly valued among men is detestable in God's sight.'"

28   Mark 13:10: "And the gospel must first be preached to all nations."

29   John 14:6: "Jesus answered, 'I am the way and the truth and the life. No one comes to the Father except through me.'"

30   Psalm 28:7: "The LORD is my strength and my shield; my heart trusts in him, and I am helped. My heart leaps for joy and I will give thanks to him in song."

Brandi McDonald Sikes, Author

Brandi McDonald Sikes is an inspirational writer, Bible teacher, and top producing commercial real estate broker. As a student of God's Word since age 7, she is inspired to illuminate the minds of children from tradition to truth.

Julia Embrey Mann, Illustrator

Julia Embrey Mann is an accomplished artist and muralist. She has always loved drawing and colored pencils. In fact, she used some of the very same colored pencils from her early childhood to create the artwork for *My Santa*. This is her first picture book. She lives in Houston, Texas, with her husband and two boys.

Visit her at **www.juliamann.squarespace.com.**

Printed in the United States
by Baker & Taylor Publisher Services